Copyright © 1993 by Editions Dessain.
First published in French as *Mon Chat et Moi* by Editions Dessain,
an imprint of De Boeck-Wesmael S. A., Avenue Louise, 203, 1050 Bruxelles.
English translation copyright © 1993 by Tambourine Books.

Library of Congress Cataloging in Publication Data

Strub, Susanne, [*Mon chat et moi*. English] My cat and I/by Susanne
Strub. —1st U.S. ed. p.cm. Translation of: *Mon chat et moi*.
Summary: A child's cat is perceived to have an enviable but not perfect life, since
the cat has a lot of freedom but not total control over what happens to him.
[1. Cats—Fiction.] I. Title—PZ7.S9258My 1993 [E]—dc20—92-21839
CIP AC ISBN 0-688-12008-3 (TR). —ISBN 0-688-12009-1 (LE)

10 9 8 7 6 5 4 3 2 1
First U.S. edition

Susanne Strub
My Cat and I

TAMBOURINE BOOKS

NEW YORK

My cat really lives the good life.

He always seems so happy.

He doesn't have to go to school

or wake up early.

He can nap all day long,

anywhere he wants to.

My cat can go for a walk
anytime he feels like it.

He never has to say where he's going…

or when he's coming back.

And no one ever makes him do homework.

But sometimes my cat gets stuck outside
because nobody's home to let him in.

When I go on vacation he has to stay with
Aunt Bertha and that's no fun for him.

And what does he eat every day of the year?

Nothing but cat food!

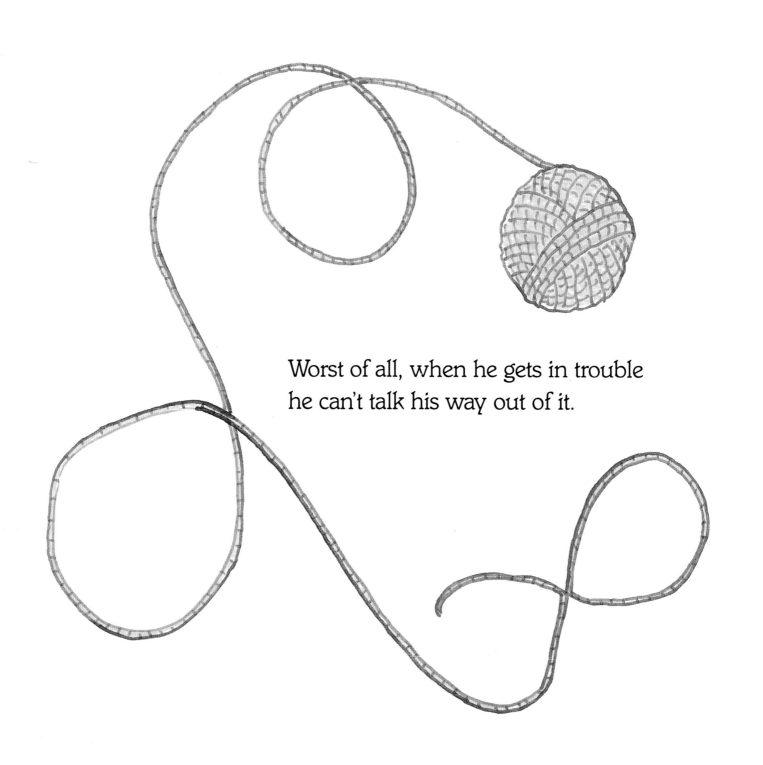

Worst of all, when he gets in trouble
he can't talk his way out of it.

I don't know which of us has the better life. But my cat and I sure are glad we have each other.